Put Your Business Online... Simply!

A GUIDE FOR ACCELERATING YOUR BUSINESS ON THE INTERNET

by
Erin Cammann
Pankaj Mayor
Rahul Razdan

Illustrated by
Anant Ahuja

TABLE OF CONTENTS

FOREWORD

The authors of this book spent several decades working in Fortune 500 companies, where we had access to products, resources and budgets that let us analyze and strategize with a great degree of sophistication about our companies, their performance, and their position in the marketplace. As we looked at the world of small business, we found that the Internet has given savvy small business owners access to similar capability at an affordable price. However, many small businesses are not taking advantage of these new opportunities. In other words, there is a gap between what is possible and what small businesses are currently doing.

This gap arises from two sources. One is a problem of awareness and understanding, and the other is a problem of application. A majority of the small business owners we have met know their business but do not appreciate all the opportunities available on the Internet. More importantly, they are unaware of new, easy-to-use tools available to help them, and they do not recognize the requirements that are being imposed by the rapidly evolving online world.

We have addressed the problem of application by creating a company—Ocoos—that provides a platform for small businesses to get online easily and utilize these Internet tools to improve marketing, sales, customer interaction and productivity.

We wrote this book to address the problem of awareness and understanding. We want to explain—in the context of small businesses—how the Internet and its resources work. Our goal is to give small business owners concrete tools to help their companies accelerate their success.

Finally, we would like to thank the following individuals for their valuable feedback: Jaye Baille, past president of Chamber of Commerce; Phil Geist, CEO Small Business Development Center, Central Florida chapter; Barbara Fitos; President of Community Foundation; Harvey Paskin, Service Corps of Retired Executives (SCORE) leader in Central Florida; and Len Horan and Luis Deschamps, who offer consulting services to small businesses.

INTRODUCTION

As the owner of a small business, you juggle multiple responsibilities every day. You try to improve your services to existing customers, you think about how to attract new customers, and you focus on improving the operations of your business. You recognize that some of your competitors and business partners are using the Internet and its resources to streamline their operations, attract new customers, and grow their businesses. And you wonder how you could do the same.

Like many other small business owners, you have not had time to learn about the Internet and how it could benefit your business. Maybe you believed the technology was too complicated for you to understand and apply to your business, or the solutions were going to be too expensive to implement. Here is the good news—the things you need to know about the Internet are fairly straightforward, and the solutions you need to use the Internet to benefit your business are easily accessible and affordable. This book will explain basic principles and terminology of the Internet, and it will provide practical, useful information designed to help you get your business online.

You have worked hard at building and running your business. However, business as usual, even for a strong and healthy company, is no longer good enough. The Internet has created a global marketplace, and it is reshaping how business is done. This is a revolution you have to join, or you will be left behind. Businesses need to be where their customers are. Customers worldwide are going online to research products and services, to make purchases, and to provide feedback. In 2012, ecommerce—or Internet-based sales—topped

$1 trillion for the first time. Given the explosive growth of the Internet, you need to use the power of this global network to keep your business competitive.

Robert owns a company in Florida that builds detached garages, which are in high demand for campers and boats. "Five years ago, we needed showrooms for people to see what we could build. Today, I do all of our business on the Internet. Customers find us online and visit our website, which lets me show more varieties of garages than I could have in one of the old showrooms. I use Facebook to generate leads from friends of my happy customers. It's a win-win for both," says Robert.

Frank sells insurance for a major insurance company. "Just in my region, there are 30 other insurance agents who sell very similar products, so differentiating myself is a huge challenge. In addition, most of my customers now look for insurance information on the Internet. I started writing educational articles and publishing them on my website. This helped me move higher in the search rankings, and also built my credibility as an expert who customers prefer to do business with," says Frank.

Jane runs a non-profit focused on children's issues. "Fundraising is a significant issue for non-profits. Accepting donations online easily and especially from people using mobile phones is very important in my business. We put a lot of effort into building up our social media presence and making sure we had a smooth payment process. As a result we have been able to grow donations in a manner which was not possible using traditional methods," says Jane.

By establishing a presence for your company online, you give target customers a means to find and engage with you on their terms. In the past, your physical storefront might have attracted the attention of anyone walking or driving down the street. Your listing in the Yellow Pages or your ad in the local paper might have gotten people to call you. But in the current era of personal computers, tablets, and the ever-present smartphones, more and more people are turning to their devices when they want information about a business. With the Internet, the world is a much smaller place and you are competing for customers on a global scale. Your business needs an online presence in order to get the attention of this group of customers.

You do not have to be a computer wizard to develop an effective online presence for your company. There are a variety of tools and services available that can help you get your business online. Some can assist you with developing a website, while others help you conduct business transactions online or help improve your productivity. This book will provide you with information to help you choose options that are most beneficial to you and your company.

Think of the Internet as the best hostess you have ever met. She is throwing a massive party, everyone is invited, and there are some amazing party favors waiting for you. All you have to do is open the door and step in.

PART 1

Your Customers Live In An Internet World

The Internet has changed the way your customers live and work, and these changes are here to stay. This is especially true in the business world. More and more traditional business actions—things like advertising, payments and customer communication—are happening "online." In other words, they are taking place on the Internet. At the same time, the global reach of the Internet has accelerated the use of new tools like online search and social networks. As a small business owner, you need to understand the new normal of doing business in order to remain competitive and be successful.

What Exactly is the Internet?

First let's talk about the basics of how the Internet works. At the most fundamental level, the Internet is a global network of computers that are connected to each other. Computers on the Internet can communicate and share information nearly instantly. No central organization manages this massive network. Anyone in the world can connect his or her computer to the Internet and be a part of the online community. Why is this important? Imagine you had access to employees who worked around the clock without complaining and who could instantly connect with your customers at any time. That is the power of the Internet from the perspective of a business owner.

With a few strokes on the keyboard or a few clicks with a mouse, your customers can explore a virtual world of nearly infinite information. People often refer to this as browsing, navigating, or surfing the web. Similar to a wave, the Internet—this "web" of interconnected computers—is fluid and constantly evolving. New sources of information are being added every second. As a member of this online community, your customers are free to visit or "surf" websites and access content from computers around the globe.

Computers connected to the Internet can send and receive data, pictures, documents, and videos. The Internet enables your customers to handle monetary transactions, provides your customers with technical assistance, and helps your customers stay in touch and communicate with their friends, family and business associates. Today, your customers can turn on their computers, pick up their smartphones, or reach for their tablets and search for, shop for, or sell nearly anything from anywhere in the world. The Internet has opened up new possibilities for everyone, and we are all learning what it means to live in the world of Google, Facebook, Yahoo and countless other websites.

What is the Impact of the Internet?

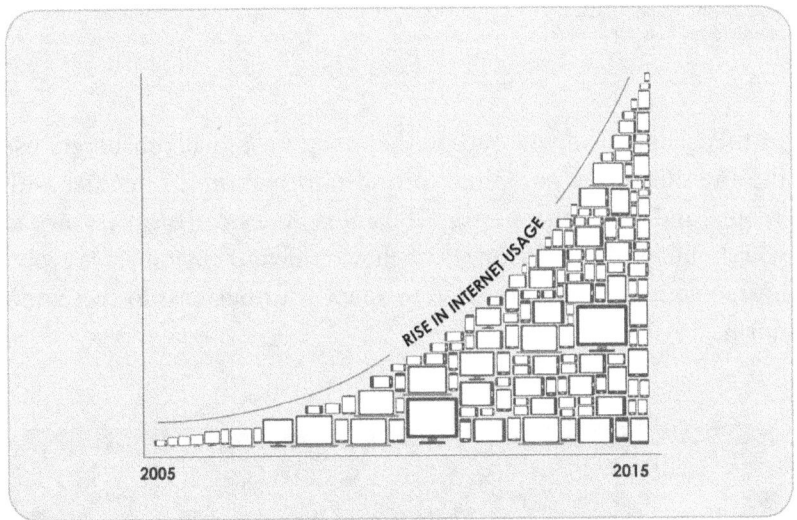

The Internet is not the first communication advance to have a widespread impact on business. We've seen it happen before. When the postal service became more reliable, companies like Sears Roebuck used catalogs to build large retail empires. The invention of the telephone changed our world by enabling people to talk to each other over vast distances, and insurance companies such as GEICO flourished by doing commerce over the phone. Similarly, the Internet is creating new opportunities to engage with consumers. We are in the early stages of this transformation, but companies such as Google and Amazon have already changed the marketplace. As we progress in the Internet age, nearly every aspect of business is likely to be transformed.

Consumer Behavior

In this chapter, we will outline the many ways that consumers use the Internet. They go online to find information, to interact with people, and to conduct personal business. As a small business owner, you should understand how the behavior of your customers is evolving, so you are better prepared to adapt your business to these new norms.

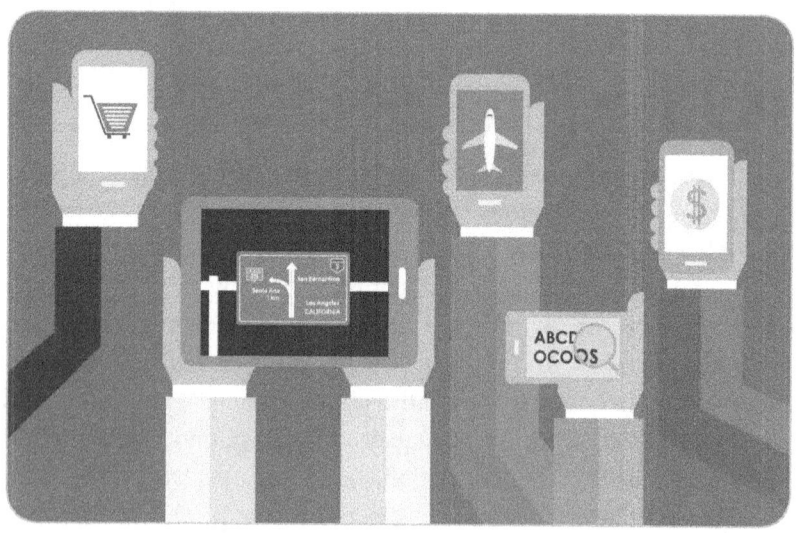

How Do Consumers Find Things Online?

The Internet is all about getting the information you want and getting it when you want it. Gone are the days of hunting through the local Yellow Pages to find a plumber when the shower won't work, or stopping by the automobile club to get maps before heading on a road trip. Now consumers turn on their computers to do a quick search for a local plumber, or type an address into their smartphones to get turn-by-turn directions to their destination. When planning their vacation, they search travel websites like Expedia or Kayak for the best deals. When staying at a hotel, they don't look for a concierge to give them a list of nearby restaurants. Instead they use websites like Yelp or Trip Advisor to find restaurants—as well as reviews and recommendations about them—on their smartphones. This immediate access to information and answers comes from three main sources: Directories, Search Engines, and Review Sites.

Directories: Directories have been the conventional means for consumers to find whatever businesses they are looking for. Traditional printed directories, which are compiled by local organizations such as the Chamber of Commerce, the local visitors center, or even a neighborhood magazine, are valuable only when they are current. The reality is that as soon as a directory is printed, it is likely to be out-of-date. New businesses open or existing ones close, phone numbers and hours of operation change, new services are added and old services are discontinued. With traditional directories, consumers risk looking up information that is no longer accurate.

In contrast to their printed counterparts, online directories can be updated at any time, making them a more reliable source of information. The Internet lets nearly anyone publish content, so directories can be as general or as specific as their creators prefer. Numerous special interest groups are now creating directories and lists that have value to people with similar interests or backgrounds. Angie's List is an online directory that provides listings and ratings of service providers in a given area. YellowPages.com is the online version of the traditional yellow pages. Manta provides a large directory of small businesses that can each "claim" and enhance their profiles.

Search Engines: Everything that is published on the Internet is searchable, so rather than browsing a directory, many people prefer to search the Internet for their specific requirements. They do so by typing what they are looking for into a search engine. The more popular search engines being used today are Google, Yahoo and Bing.

Search engines exist to give consumers answers. So how do they find those answers? A search engine like Google maintains an index of the information available on the Internet, just like a library catalogs all the books in its system. This process of building an index is called web crawling. A search engine's computers continually "crawl" the Internet, visiting websites, following the links within those websites to other websites, and cataloging all this information. The search engine later sorts through this data and indexes it. When you type what you are looking for into a search engine, the engine looks through its indexes and nearly instantly finds and displays websites that it considers useful to you.

Today, a major search engine will index hundreds of millions of pages and respond to tens of millions of queries every day. This new concept of searching the Internet has not only changed the way we look for answers, it has transformed our vocabulary. What do you do when you need to know the answer to something? Chances are you Google it!

Review Sites: If online directories and search engines let you discover businesses online, review sites on the Internet let you know what you can expect from these businesses. Traditional media sources such as newspapers, magazines, and radio or television news programs have in-house experts to report on subjects like new books, movies, plays, music, hotels, and restaurants. Online review sites have fundamentally altered this landscape. Now anyone can review anything and publish an opinion online. The Internet has enabled people to give voice to their inner critic. Want to tell people about a restaurant you just tried? You can post your comments on Yelp. Enthusiastic about the country inn you visited last week with your spouse? You can tell other would-be romantics about it on Trip Advisor.

Online review sites let us read the opinions and experiences of hundreds of other consumers just like us. The collective wisdom provided by this "crowd sourcing" has proven to be very persuasive. A restaurant critic for the local newspaper might praise the new burger joint across town without convincing us to visit it. But when hundreds of people online agree that they have never tasted better French fries or a richer milkshake than at that same burger joint, we might decide to give it a try. Similarly if one traditional reviewer says he was unimpressed with a new hotel, readers might think he was being overly critical. But if the majority of online reviewers complain of surly staff members, drafty windows and uncomfortable beds, we will probably look for lodgings elsewhere.

Online reviews have become so effective that many merchants now choose to incorporate customer reviews on their websites. The best-known examples of this are provided by the online superstore Amazon and the auction site EBay. When you are shopping for something on Amazon, you can look for popular items, read the reviews from other consumers, and see what people looking for similar things have purchased. On EBay you can read reviews and see ratings of the sellers. This allows you to make informed decisions on the reliability of vendors and their claims before you decide to buy from them.

How Do People Interact With Each Other Online?

Computers, tablets and smartphones are doing such a good job connecting people online that communication is becoming an increasingly virtual experience. Consumers no longer have to see or hear

whomever they are talking to. People still chat with their neighbors, they still phone their friends, but increasing they send someone an email, post a status update, send a text, or tweet about the latest news. Online communication is booming in a world of email, instant messaging, and social networks.

Email: Twenty years ago, only academic institutions and a few technology businesses communicated by email. Now everyone—from young children to great-grandparents—has discovered the benefits of sending mail electronically. Several characteristics of email contribute to its popularity. Unlike regular mail, it is delivered instantly, but unlike a telephone call, you can respond at your convenience. Email costs nothing to send, it can be accessed from any computer or mobile device, and it can be sent to more than one person at the same time. Email addresses are now on everything from business cards and resumes to the roster of your child's sports team and the staff directory at your neighborhood school. Email has become a preferred method for personal communication. Its use is growing in everyday commerce as well.

Instant Messaging/Texting: Some people don't want to wait for their friends to check for new emails. They want their friends to see their messages immediately. Instant messages and text messages deliver content directly to the screens of the recipients. Teenagers especially have embraced the immediate nature of texting and instant messaging. At any given time, they are likely to be conducting multiple parallel conversations using their phones.

The increasing use of mobile devices is blurring the lines between instant messaging on a computer and texting on a phone. A good example is iMessage from Apple, which allows consumers to send and receive messages to other users of Apple devices, whether they are on a laptop, a desktop computer, an iPad, or an iPhone. Another example is WhatsApp, which enables consumers to send and receive messages from different types of mobile devices.

Social Networks: You may not have thought of it in these terms, but we are all part of many different social networks. A social network is any group of people having distinct and common interests. You might belong to a gym, be part of a book club, or be active in a church group. Maybe you have joined your local wildlife association or a museum society, or you are a member of your town's Chamber of Commerce. These are all social networks. And like their real-world counterparts, social networks that exist online have their own identities and norms of behavior.

Social networks can be powerful tools to benefit your business. But in order to take advantage of these opportunities, you need to understand a little bit about the general characteristics of the networks. Some networks, like Facebook, are informal, social gathering places. Others networks, like LinkedIn, help people in the business world find and connect with people of similar professional interests. Still others are defined more by their content than their constituents. Twitter, for example, limits all users to messages of only 140 characters or less.

You can see the influence of online social networks all around you. Twitter is fast replacing traditional sources for breaking news; you may hear about an accident, a sports score, or an election result from a post on Twitter before you hear about it through traditional news media. Facebook has been used to organize mass protests and even—in some countries—revolutions. And in the business world, social networks give you access to a scale of audience that was previously impossible to reach.

These social networks provide different capabilities for businesses to interact with consumers. For example, Facebook lets people create home pages for their companies. These home pages are called "fan pages," and they enable you to promote your business on Facebook, alert people who are interested in your business about upcoming events, and build your social network. In addition, when you advertise through social networks like Facebook, you can target your audience based on a range of characteristics such as age, location, interests and recent search history.

How Do People Interact With Businesses Online?

In addition to changing the norms of personal communication, the Internet has impacted how consumers interact with businesses. Your customers don't have to speak to a live person to find out what they want to know. Gone are the days of waiting for an office or store to open so a customer can call or drop in to get information. When consumers want to buy something, they expect to be able to go online, find their product, read a few reviews about it, send an email if they have a question, and make their purchase. We live in the age of instantaneous access, and the Internet is always open for business. More often than not, if what you offer is not easily accessible online, consumers will take their business elsewhere.

Customers today expect—and often demand—an online presence from businesses with whom they interact. Companies that meet or exceed their customers' online expectations are more likely to be successful. The ones that do not do so will find themselves fighting to stay competitive in an increasingly online world.

Business Behavior: Marketing in an Online World

In this chapter, we will first discuss the basics of marketing. Within this framework, we will talk about how the Internet offers many capabilities that can be used to market your business, and we will discuss search engines and online advertising in greater detail.

Marketing Basics

What is marketing? Your business has something to offer. It might be a service or it might be a physical product. Your business will exist only if there are customers willing to pay for what you offer.

Marketing is the process by which you identify potential customers, communicate the value of your product or service to them, and turn them into paying clients. The "Four P's" of marketing—Product, Place, Price, and Promotion—help you with this process.

Product: This is the product or service that you are selling. It is the solution you are offering to meet a customer's need. Having the right product is the first step to building a successful business.

Product questions you need to address:

1. *What value do you offer to the customer, and what customer need does it meet?*
2. *What is unique about what you offer, and who would be most likely to need it?*
3. *Is it a necessity or a luxury?*
4. *Whom are you trying to sell to? And who is offering products similar to yours?*

Promotion: When you first think of marketing, you most likely think about how to promote your product. By understanding the behavior of your target customers, you will be able to advertise and sell to them more effectively and efficiently. Traditional promotional tools include product literature, billboards, commercials, print ads, and directory listings. Promoting your product provides potential customers with information about your product and increases their awareness about the availability and value of your product.

Promotion questions you need to address:

1. *How do you communicate to people about your company and your product?*
2. *Where will potential customers go to find information about your product, and how can you increase your visibility in these places?*
3. *What is the most cost-effective way to educate people about your product?*

Price: "How much does it cost?" is one of the first questions most consumers ask. You need to set a price that positions your product or service competitively in the market and provides you with a reasonable profit. Sometimes price can convey an impression about the quality of your product; a low price may give an impression of lower quality, but a high price might place your product out of reach for a segment of your target market. Setting a price for your product is a critical decision that needs to balance multiple, oftentimes conflicting, criteria.

Price questions you need to address:

1. *What do people expect to pay for similar products?*
2. *Is there sufficient differentiation to price your product higher than competing products?*
3. *Will a lower price significantly increase the volume of sales?*

Place: This refers to your distribution channel, or how you get your products to your customer. In retail, some companies (such as Gap, Levi's, and Apple) sell their products in their own stores, while others use large department stores such as Target or Walmart as retail distributors. Place determines how a customer is able to gain access to your product.

Place questions you need to address:

1. *Where do your target customers go to look for a product like yours?*
2. *Do you sell your product or service directly to consumers, or do you use a distribution/retail channel?*

The Four P's are not steps taken in sequence to determine a marketing strategy. Instead they are related components that, working together, will help you grow your business. They provide a framework for building your overall marketing strategy. The Four P's should not be looked at one time and then set aside. The market changes, and so does your marketing strategy. By continually evaluating the Four P's of marketing, you will give your business the best chance of creating and maintaining its competitive edge.

While the Internet has impacted all four of these components of marketing, the areas of place and promotion have undergone the most change. Now we will cover these two aspects in more detail.

Online Advertising: Targeting Your Customer

Traditional advertising sought to divert your attention from whatever you may have been doing at that time. Commercials interrupted the program you were watching on television, print advertisements sought to attract your attention away from the article you were reading, billboards and flyers tried to grab your eye as you were walking down the street or driving down the road. Interruption was not always pleasant for the consumer, and companies could not be sure if their target audience was paying attention to their ads and being influenced by them. Sure, an athletic shoe company could pay for ad time during a football game and a cosmetics company could buy a spot in a beauty magazine, but those companies would never know if the people seeing their ads were interested in new running shoes or the season's hottest shade of lipstick. In contrast, the impact of advertising on the Internet can be measured, so you can refine and increase the effectiveness of your marketing strategy.

The growth in the use of the Internet has modified consumer behavior and consequently impacted how we think about place and promotion of our products. Because customers now make buying decisions based on information they gather through online searches, it is no longer sufficient to get the attention of consumers with a message we hope is appropriate, timely, and compelling. Instead, knowing that consumers will seek out information they are interested in, you can reach them while they are researching a related topic. And once you get their attention, you can inform them about your business, your products and your services, and then ultimately convince them to make a purchase.

A common form of advertising on the Internet is through the use of web banners or banner ads. A banner ad is an advertisement embedded in a webpage. Banner ads appear on webpages alongside the main content of the page, in much the same way magazine advertisements are placed next to the editorial content of a page. These ads either appear across the top of the screen or are placed at strategic places on a webpage. If your ad catches their interest, customers can click on it and go directly to a page on your business's website.

With online advertising, you are able to get immediate feedback about the effectiveness of your advertising campaign. You can set up banners ads to be displayed on webpages that relate to your product. As people view or click through your ads online, measurement and tracking tools gather data and provide you detailed information about the audience. You get access to demographic data as well as more specific profile data about individual people and their interests, shopping habits, and browsing history.

In addition to placing your ad on a specific website and hoping that appropriate people notice it, you can also target specific consumers and have your ads appear on webpages they are currently browsing. In the first case, a running shoe company might place a banner ad on a website providing advice to potential marathon runners. In the second situation, a business that runs adventure tours in Maui can have its ads placed on pages being viewed by anyone who is searching for Hawaiian vacations.

Companies that support advertising on the Internet or digital advertising can help you create and place your ads in the most effective way. You can run different ads on the same webpage and determine which ones generate the most activity. These companies offer you the ability to track and measure the effectiveness of your advertising campaign in real time.

Search Engine Optimization: Fighting For Position

With advertising, you are trying to get the attention of a customer who is engaged in doing something else. This approach can have mixed results. In some situations it may be more effective to have customers discover your business on their own when they are searching for the products and services they need.

In a fraction of a second, a search engine like Google or Yahoo can provide a customer with thousands of possible websites to visit. Having your website appear at the top of the search list could significantly increase the number of customers who visit your website and purchase your product.

But how can you improve your business's website position on that list? The process of improving the ranking of a webpage in the results of a search request is known as Search Engine Optimization (SEO), and it is a key element that can impact the success of your online marketing efforts.

Search engines look primarily for content, and they order their results based on the relevancy of the content. Consumers can increase the likelihood of getting useful results by being more specific in their search requests. Searching for "gardeners" generates more than eight million results. But searching for "gardeners Los Angeles" brings the results down to a little under two million.

Still, two million? This is not a helpful list for anyone. To provide more useful results from the search, search engines rank websites. First they try to match for content. If a user is looking for restaurants and the content on a specific webpage indicates it is a restaurant, search engines will consider it a good match. Search engines also give higher rankings to websites that are trusted. This means that sites administered by a governmental department or some other agency with authority, websites that have multiple links to and from many other websites, and websites with fresh, frequently updated content will rank higher.

Some data associated with a website is not visible on the web page but can still be seen by a search engine. If this invisible data, or meta-data, matches a search request, search engines will think they have found a good match. Given the increase in number of searches from mobile devices, when a search request comes from a mobile device, some search engines prioritize websites that are mobile optimized. By being aware of these criteria, savvy business owners can modify their website's structure and content to improve its ranking in search engine results.

While the technology of the search engines is complex, the reality for you as a small business owner is simple: if your business does not appear on the first page of the results of a requested search, potential customers will probably not find you. Early search engine optimization was all about trying to "game" the system, as people tried different tricks to improve their search ranking. Search engines are continually working to identify these tricks and avoid being gamed. As a small business owner, you should put your energy into enhancing your website's structure and content to improve its ranking in search results.

Search Engine Advertising: Paid and Organic Search

Users give search engines the keywords used to conduct searches. Basic or unassisted search is known as "organic search," and it provides results based on natural information such as relevancy and popularity. In addition, search engines such as Google have a concept known as "paid search."

When displaying search results on their web pages, search engines place paid search results above organic search results. Much like you would pay for a banner ad to appear on a webpage, you can pay for your website information to appear at the top of a list of search results. Instead of buying an advertising spot, you bid on specific keywords.

When the keywords you pay for are entered in a search request and your bid is high enough, your company's website will appear higher in the search results page.

Next time you conduct a web search using Google, take a moment to look at the webpage displaying your search results. See if you can distinguish the break between paid search results, which will appear at the top of the page, and organic search results, which will be lower down on the page. If you weren't looking for it, would you notice the difference? Or would you just scan down the list of results and try to determine which one looked like the best fit for your needs?

If your company serves a specific niche and your customers are likely to enter keywords that will bring them straight to you, you probably don't need to explore the benefits of paid search. But if you are one of many players in a crowded industry, paid search could help you get the attention of potential customers.

Edward restores antique Mercedes-Benz cars in Durham, North Carolina. "I am fortunate because I am the only guy in town who specializes in antique Benz's," he says. Edwards's potential customers are likely to type something like "antique Mercedes-Benz restoration Durham" in a search. "I have a pretty good website, and people seem to find me when they search for someone to help them with their cars," he says. "I try to update the information on my website frequently, but I don't think I need to pay for special keywords. However, I would like to get some other car businesses or Mercedes dealerships to link to my website."

Debbie is one of many personal trainers in Portland, Oregon. "Portland is pretty health-conscious," she says. "There are a lot of other personal trainers around, and I know I need to have a good website to attract new customers. I update my site with content about healthy living and healthy lifestyles, but everyone else is doing the same thing on their websites, too. It is worth the expense to me to pay for some search keywords so that people see my website first when they look for a trainer."

Business Behavior: Finance in an Online World

CHAPTER

3

Finance and payments are critical aspects for any business. We will first cover basic concepts for analyzing the financial health of your business. We will then expand our scope to look at the financial tools that are available to you online. Some of these tools are designed to help you understand and keep track of your business. Other tools can help you accept payments online.

Finance Basics

At the core of any business is an exchange of value—either a product or a service—for monetary compensation. The sum of all such transactions is your business.

The three main ways to track your company's financial health are:

1. Balance Sheets
2. Profit and Loss Statements
3. Cash Flow

Balance sheets: A business's balance sheet shows its assets and liabilities at a given moment in time. An asset could be cash, it could be inventory, and it could be a piece of equipment. It is anything that counts toward a company's worth at that instant. A liability is anything that will negatively impact the company's ability to continue operating. Debt is a liability, as are unpaid bills. If you have performed a service or sold a product and you are still waiting to be paid, that outstanding balance is considered an asset (or "accounts receivable" in accounting terms).

Profit and loss: While a balance sheet is a view of your company's business at a specific instant in time, a profit and loss statement details your company's financial health over a specific period of time. Profit and Loss—also called P&L—statements track the amount of money coming into your company and the amount of money going out of it. Your profit margin—or the money you actually make—is the difference between the two. P&L statements will give you a sense of the rhythm of your business. Do you have periods of peak activity followed by quiet spells? Can you reliably predict when you will be busy and when you will be slow, and can you consequently be prepared for both?

Cash flow: As the name implies, cash flow tracks the movement of cash into and out of your company. For a small business owner, cash flow is critical because it determines whether or not you can pay your bills. For example, consider the case of the "land rich, cash poor farmer." Old MacDonald might have a lot of assets, but if he doesn't have cash on hand, he won't be able to pay his utility bill. Similarly, if you have sold your goods or services but your customers have not yet paid for them, your P&L statement might look good, but you won't have cash to pay your rent.

You can apply these financial tools to understanding and planning your business's financial operations. With this information, you can determine the profitability of your different business offerings, you can identify what kind of cash flow to expect, and you can figure out how that impacts the working capital you need in the bank to keep your business operating successfully.

Online Financial Tools

Large businesses spend a great deal of time and energy managing and examining their financial transactions. They have the resources to do so, and they know that understanding their business operations helps them improve those operations. Until recently, these tools were custom-developed or required financial experts to do the analysis. Over the past few years, many software programs have been developed to help small business owners manage all aspects of their businesses' finances without having to hire teams of finance experts.

There are some excellent tools available online for handling the finances for your business. You need to pay your employees, your vendors and your suppliers. You also need to track how much you owe the IRS in taxes. With products like those offered by Intuit and Freshbooks, you can easily:

1. **Track Payments:** Categorize your budget items and build awareness of where the money in your business is coming from and where it is being spent.
2. **Track Invoices:** Know which customer has paid and whose payment is still outstanding.
3. **Manage Payroll:** Organize payment of wages and salaries, communicate with the IRS and state revenue departments, and create W-2s and withholdings.
4. **Manage payments to consultants:** Create 1099s.

Online Payments

If you are selling something, then you need to make sure your customers can buy it. If you have a physical storefront, this probably means you already accept cash, checks, or credit and debit cards. If your business has an Internet storefront, you need to decide what forms of payment you will accept online. Customers will often have their preferred method of payment, and they will expect you to be able to accept it.

Many options are available to allow you to accept various forms of payment online. Customers often prefer to use credit cards and debit cards for their smallest transactions. They may use checks or electronic funds transfers for larger transactions, and they may use online payments systems for smaller transactions. PayPal and Google Wallet are two of the more popular online payment systems. They allow for the secure storage of credit card or bank account details, enabling the customer to pay for online purchases.

In the past, moving from a cash-only business to one that supported different payment types could be expensive and cumbersome. You had to develop a relationship with a bank, set up a merchant account, and figure out how to support electronic fund transfers. If you wanted to handle credit card transactions, you had to buy an expensive Point-of-Sales (POS) System from Visa or MasterCard. This process was time consuming and expensive. Some small business owners chose not to go through it, resulting in a loss of potential revenue.

Many companies now offer platforms that help you manage payments in forms convenient to you and your customer. These platforms have helped eliminate the high initial costs that used to be associated with online payments, making online payments more accessible.

Point-of-Sale transactions (POS): Services like Square or Intuit's GoPayment provide you with a device that connects to most mobile phones and allows you to swipe credit cards and accept payment.

Online Payments: Services like PayPal and Google Wallet make is easy for customers to send you funds without the need for a credit card.

Checks and electronic funds transfers: While you still need a bank to handle these transactions, most banks now have easy-to-use Internet portals for depositing checks and enabling electronic transfers.

The Internet levels the playing field for managing finances, and small businesses like yours now have affordable access to some of the same capabilities that larger businesses use for financial management and reporting. These products have improved small companies' financial capabilities in the same way FedEx and UPS improved their logistics. These financial tools have made it possible for small business owners to claim their rightful spots in the Internet's global marketplace.

Business Behavior: Productivity in an Online World

In this chapter, we will first talk about what it means to be productive and to improve your productivity. Before we start, we should point out that small businesses need to worry more about productivity than large businesses. Why? Small businesses face the same fixed costs as large businesses, but they have much less margin for error. Thus we will look at some ways the Internet can help you become more productive.

Productivity Basics

When people talk about your business's productivity, they don't merely refer to the goods you produce. Productivity is a measurement that compares input (labor, costs, materials, and time) versus output (finished products and revenue). Businesses that increase their productivity either produce more for the same cost or produce the same for less cost, and hence they are able to be more profitable.

Businesses can improve their productivity by analyzing the process by which they bring their goods to market and then looking for ways to become more efficient in that process. Some common strategies for improving productivity include: improving workers' capabilities through training, making supply chain and distribution changes, and finding technological advances that aid in production.

Improving Your Productivity Online

There are many ways in which the Internet can help you increase your productivity. How many times have you shuffled through a pile of papers or rifled through your desk trying to find a specific piece of information about a client? Have you ever driven halfway to a meeting only to realize you left an important spreadsheet in a file at your office? Has an unexpected opportunity presented itself and you realized that you didn't have the information you needed on hand?

Using the Internet gives you ready access to all your pertinent information from wherever you happen to be. When your back office exists online, files don't get misplaced, and they don't get forgotten at the office while you are on the road. They are with you whenever you bring along your smartphone or computer. You can use the Internet to make your business practices smoother and more efficient, thereby making your company more competitive and more profitable.

The Internet has been called "the great equalizer" for its ability to level the playing field for smaller companies. Internet technology has been evolving rapidly, and many small businesses have yet to take advantage of all the value it has to offer. There are four main classes of online tools that help increase your company's productivity. They are:

1. Content Generation/Management
2. Tools in the Cloud
3. Communication
4. Online Scheduling

Content Generation and Management

Over the last 30 years, more and more people are putting away pen and paper and turning on their computers when they need to create content. Computers can assist you with bookkeeping and financial analysis, with invoicing, with preparing documents for publication, and with creating slides and graphics for presentations. They provide you with spell checkers, built-in fonts, and built-in drawing packages, letting you create professional-looking documents quickly and easily. They allow you to update, copy, search for, store, and back up your documents.

The other important content generation tools are your friendly digital cameras, tablets, and smartphones. Today, people use these to produce text, video, music and graphics that can be posted online and linked to a business's website. In the past you could only use these tools on your computer at your desk. The Internet enables you to be able to create and manage content online from any device you choose.

Overall, these innovations provide small businesses with the capabilities to generate and manage content that will compete in look and professionalism with that of larger businesses with many more resources at their disposal.

Tools in the Cloud

Most productivity tools are available to you "in the cloud." What exactly does this mean? Before the Internet became so pervasive, your personal computer stored all the programs and data you needed to do your work. This model had its advantages, as all you needed was an outlet to plug in your computer, and you could access all your programs and data.

This model of operation also had many disadvantages. You needed to buy tools like Microsoft Excel from retail stores like Staples and install them on your computer. The content generated from these tools was stored either on your hard drive or on removable disks or drives. This meant you as a small business owner became responsible for all the technical issues related to your computers. You had to:

1. Maintain up-to-date versions of the software programs.
2. Back up critical data in case of physical issues with your computer.
3. Make sure data was stored securely.
4. Figure out how to transport data to other computers and devices.

All this was a distraction from your main goal—managing and growing your business. The "cloud" addresses these issues by moving hardware (computers), software (programs) and data to large, professionally managed service providers.

The backbone of the so-called cloud is provided by enormous datacenters run by companies like IBM and Amazon. They offer you computing resources, so you don't need to purchase and continually update your own hardware. Additionally, your own devices do not have to be so powerful, as the computers in the cloud do the heavy computing. The software you need on the cloud comes from companies like Intuit, Ocoos, Freshbooks, Google and Microsoft, and instead of buying this software and loading it onto your own computer, you buy the Software as a Service (also known as SaaS), which you utilize through the cloud. Companies like Dropbox, Google, Amazon or Microsoft provide data storage on the cloud. You can now purchase hardware, software and storage resources individually or as a bundled service.

When your programs and data are stored on the cloud, you have easy access to whatever information you need from any device, and you aren't responsible for maintenance, backup or security. Using cloud-based solutions, you can focus on using the capabilities you need to run your business without worrying about technology support issues. If you need more hardware, it is easy to upgrade. If the software changes, you automatically get the new version. And additional storage is only a click away.

Cloud-based services also lower your upfront fixed costs. You don't need to buy computers and software—instead you can purchase what you need for the time you need it and in the volume you need it. By providing these services in volume, the cloud providers are able to lower their costs and often pass on the savings to you.

The bottom line is that cloud-based services increase your productivity, lower your cost and take the hassle out of technology. They free you to focus more of your attention on growing your business.

Cathy runs a boat rental service. "I can manage my entire business with my laptop. Customers schedule their rentals and make payments for them online, I send them detailed directions via email, and they sign legal documents with a digital signature. All my financial data is in the cloud, so I can get to it from my computer or my iPhone."

Communication

As it has with content generation and management, the Internet has revolutionized communication. While some communication still is best delivered on paper in an envelope by the post office, email has replaced the letter in most business settings. It is a low cost—sometimes no-cost—way to communicate instantly throughout the business world. Letters can be sent via email, and so can pictures, videos, spreadsheets, and large documents. Automated mass email programs and email tracking software enable you to run email-marketing campaigns, provide you with tools to analyze consumer response to

those campaigns, and then let you tailor your message based on that response.

Voice-over-internet protocol (VOIP) services such as Skype and WebEx are growing quickly and changing the way we speak to people. Remember the days of worrying about long-distance telephone charges? VOIP services turn your computer into a phone line and let you communicate with clients near and far for minimal or no charge. This technology also offers you additional communication capabilities. You can set up and conduct conference calls through your computer with WebEx and Skype, and you can run online meetings with Join.me or Screenleap, which lets you invite participants to see the images on your computer screen. These tools provide you useful features to communicate effectively with your customers.

Online Scheduling

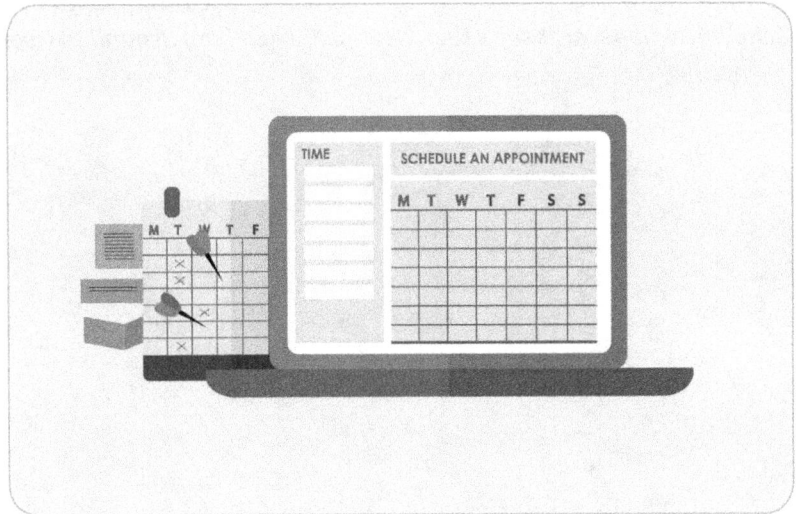

If you are a small business owner, you are often juggling the demands of speaking with clients, scheduling appointments and needing to be on the road or at work conducting your business. You either have to hire someone to handle scheduling for you or accept that you won't always be free to talk to customers when they call for an appointment, and some of these potential customers may take their business elsewhere. Integrated online platforms like those offered by Ocoos, or dedicated tools like Bookfresh and Appointy, have automated the scheduling process, letting clients see your availability and select an appointment time that is most convenient for them.

Susan, a hair stylist, used to stop working on a customer to answer calls and schedule future appointments. "I felt like my phone would always ring when I was in the middle of giving someone a hair wash—I didn't want to leave my client sitting with shampoo in her hair, but I also didn't want to miss out on booking appointments with another customer," says Susan. "Now I have my clients schedule their own appointments online, and it's been great for everyone. It certainly is easier for me, and I also feel like my business has actually increased, because people can schedule whenever it suits them, not just when I am around to take their calls."

PART 2

Taking Advantage of the Online World

Businesses need to go where the customers are going, and consumers worldwide are going online. As consumers look to the Internet for information, you should join the forward-thinking people that are using the power of this global network to grow their businesses. The Internet can benefit your business in eight main ways.

- **The Internet gains you entrance to a global marketplace.**

  The Internet has created a global marketplace. Having an Internet storefront provides a means for today's consumers to find and engage with you on their terms. Your physical storefront may attract the attention of anyone walking or driving down the street. However your online storefront can attract the attention of literally everyone who owns a personal computer, tablet or mobile phone.

- **The Internet improves your productivity.**

  You sleep. Your employees sleep. Your customers sleep. But your website never sleeps. You should be rushing to take advantage of this tireless worker who will perform reliably, quickly, and correctly the tasks you assign to it.

- **The Internet provides you with a round-the-clock storefront.**

  Consumers expect information when they want it and where they want it. They may look for it when they are on their laptops in the office, or on their tablets while lounging in bed, or on their smartphones during their commutes. They want to be able to conduct business at their convenience, and they expect you to have an online storefront that is always open to them.

  Whether your website is providing information about your products and services to prospective customers, taking and fulfilling orders, or getting customer feedback to improve your product on service, it will always be open for business. And your clients could be just around the corner or on the other side of the world.

- **The Internet automates and expands the power of "word-of-mouth" references.**

  People used to ask their friends and neighbors for advice about a good restaurant, or a reliable plumber, or the best place to go for a massage. These word-of-mouth recommendations carry a great deal of weight, but they are unreliable for you as a business owner. In order to benefit from word-of-mouth recommendations, you must first have someone physically encounter a satisfied customer of yours, and then you must have your business come up in their conversation. This does happen, but it is a slow and unpredictable process.

The Internet automates "word-of-mouth" recommendations and accelerates their impact. One good online review of your business could be read by thousands of potential customers.

■ **The Internet helps you analyze your business.**
Big corporations have departments whose function is to generate reports to understand customer behavior. They track foot traffic outside their stores. They count how many people make it inside, how many of them make a purchase, and what items are getting the most interest. Although small businesses have a sense of some of these numbers, they usually lack the resources to quantify them or measure the results of a marketing campaign. When you establish a presence for your business online, the software you use can track all this information for you automatically. This enables you to gather large volumes of data, analyze it, and get a more objective understanding of your business. Armed with this knowledge, you can take action.

■ **The Internet lets you compete on equal footing with companies of larger size and resources.**
The Internet is a great equalizer. Earlier in the book we compared it to a hostess throwing a fantastic party and we encouraged you to open the door and join in. We forgot to mention that this hostess is greeting all her guests with open arms and welcoming them with the same enthusiasm. Big companies and small companies can look the same online, where there aren't any fancy storefronts or trendy downtown street addresses to impress consumers. Your products and your services drive your success, allowing you to

compete effectively with companies of vastly larger scale and resources. Bigger isn't better online. Better is better.

- **The Internet protects your data.**

  Have you ever had your computer "crash" or had your laptop stolen, and have you lost valuable company information as a result? In the past, data needed to be manually backed up, and sometimes people didn't back up their data as often as they needed to. Today, with cloud-based applications and data storage, you do not worry about this. Someone else can take responsibility for backing up your data and keeping it secure.

- **The Internet helps you find skills you do not have in-house.**

  With marketplaces such Elance or Alibaba, the Internet can help connect you to a global network of specialists in areas ranging from design services to manufacturing services.

Website Development

We have covered the ways the Internet is changing how we live and work. Now it is time to take action. You are ready to start building a website for your business. In this chapter, we will lay out the options available to help you create your website, as well as the questions you should ask yourself about what your website should do. We will explain how to improve your website's visibility to search engines, and consequently how to improve its rank in search results.

Total Cost of Ownership

Before you invest in any new project, it is important to assess the total cost of ownership. Initial or start-up costs are not the only expenses to keep in mind. Depending on the scope and complexity of your project, you will need to plan for the costs of implementation, maintenance, and future enhancements. If you are building a house, you might choose higher quality materials that cost more up front in order to save on long-term maintenance costs. If you are getting a new car, you might buy a more expensive one that has a track record of requiring low maintenance, or you might lease a cheaper model if you plan to keep it for a few years. Similarly, when you set out to build a website, you need to keep in mind more than your initial costs.

When you create a website for your business, you are implicitly committed to the ongoing costs of maintaining that website. You will need to stay abreast of new technologies—either new devices like smartphones and tablets, or new capabilities such as handling online payments—and their impact on how consumers access and use the Internet. The choices you make when building your website will impact the future costs—in terms of both time and financial resources—of maintaining your website.

There are opportunity costs associated as well with the choices you make. You may want to have the capability to update the content of your website frequently to highlight new services, feature new promotions, showcase new references, or demonstrate momentum to prospective clients. You don't want to risk seeing a business opportunity go to a competitor because you couldn't get your website updated in time.

Your website has to be effective. Have you ever opened a website that did not display properly? Perhaps the graphic overlaid the text or the scroll bar did not work. Some of these problems may have been created because the website was not compatible with the web browser you were using. Your website should be designed to work with multiple versions of the popular browsers. In addition, as more and more people use mobile devices for browsing the Internet (almost 60 percent of web searches are done on mobile devices), your website should be "mobile friendly."

You also should consider being an active member of the online business community, in which complementary businesses link to each other's websites and provide references and recommendations to each other's business. Aligning your marketing efforts with those of your business partners can be very effective in increasing the visibility of your business. Linking between businesses, especially with positive references from other businesses, is one of the most effective ways to market your business. In order to do this, your website's infrastructure needs to be compatible with that used in the websites of your business partners. How you—and your business partners—create your websites will impact how quickly you will be able to update your content and how effortlessly you will be able to collaborate with each other online.

Web Designers, Toolkits, and Platforms

Keeping in mind all these costs, how do you go about building a website? There are currently three main approaches to creating a website for your company. You can hire a web developer, you can use an online toolkit offered by companies like GoDaddy or Web.com, or you can use an online platform offered by companies like Ocoos.

Each option has its pros and cons. Before making a choice, you should list all the capabilities you need for your online storefront and then balance these against your total budget for the website. At the very least, the website you create has to communicate with your target customers about your products and services, and it needs to provide your contact information. Do you also want the website to help you run the business? You can set up the website to take care of some scheduling and bookkeeping, and you can also use it to help you with distribution. Do you want to use the website as a tool for analysis?

If so, you can set it up to collect information about your clients and their buying preferences.

Web Designers and Mass Customization

A popular method of website development involves mass customization. You may think that your website should not be like any others. Uniqueness can be a differentiator, but it can also lead to increased cost without a noticeable benefit for your business. When appropriate, using free content management software such as Wordpress and Drupal can help you create and manage a custom-built website. You can either use pre-defined templates to help you create webpages, or you can build webpages from scratch to meet the specific requirements of your business. The end result will be a website designed to meet your needs.

If this sounds challenging to you, you can hire web designers to build your website. A web designer will be able to help you make sure your website has the capabilities you desire. You provide the requirements, and they provide the expertise. But be aware that hiring web designers can be expensive.

You should also think about how you will maintain the website once it is built. Will you continue to be dependent on your web designer for all future changes and updates to your website? And if so, how quickly can you expect your designer to take action? In today's business environment, you want to retain control of your content and be able to update your website with new information about your products and services or about new promotions whenever you need to do so—waiting for external help could produce an unwanted delay.

Toolkits

Another method for mass customization comes from using the "web builder" toolkits offered by companies like GoDaddy, Web. com, Vistaprint, Wix, and Weebly. These tools make it easier for you to develop your own website, and they often come with lower upfront costs. However, they are not very different from the previous approach. In essence, they deliver the capability for "mass customization" of websites without the need for hiring a web designer.

These web builder toolkits are well suited for building websites that don't change very much or those that are useful for a short period of time. Many people create websites for major life events like weddings and funerals, and the templates from these toolkits work well for those purposes. If you don't need your website to do much more than tell people how to find your physical business, the toolkit approach could be good for you.

The tools in these kits are inexpensive in the short term and work effectively for personal websites or websites with limited functionality, but they are less effective for small businesses desiring more capabilities. The web builder toolkits have limited ability to provide a scalable solution for a small business wanting to create an online storefront. They may have limitations in enabling easy ecommerce solutions, or have limited ability to help you with online scheduling. Adding these capabilities will require significant investment, and your total cost of ownership could increase appreciably.

Platforms

When deciding how to build your website, you might want to consider using a fully featured online platform. For a small business, using a functional platform can provide an effective and scalable way to create and manage your web presence. These platforms don't just make operating online easier; they make operating everywhere easier.

In addition to providing you an online storefront, they also help you manage some of the functions of running your business. They provide you an affordable and easily maintainable web presence that can evolve well with new technologies. Neither the custom-design model nor the toolkit approach will give you this ability. Examples of successful platforms include Facebook, Ocoos, LinkedIn, Amazon and Ebay.

An additional benefit to using a platform is that it can provide technology insurance at a relatively low cost. For example, when a new mobile device type is introduced or a new social networking tool becomes commonly used, the platform will typically handle the details and not require you to spend scarce time and resources understanding and deploying the new technology.

Jen runs a dance studio in Cleveland, Ohio, where she teaches classes seven days a week. She wanted to create a basic website that allowed for online scheduling, ecommerce, and e-signatures for liability agreements. "When I started talking to web developers, I couldn't believe how expensive everything was. And they warned me that there might be issues handling people calling from their mobile phones. I checked out GoDaddy, but it seemed like it wasn't going to be able to do everything I wanted. I finally wound up creating a page on Facebook and also using Ocoos for ecommerce and scheduling. So far it is working out really well."

Content and Capabilities

Once you have decided which method of website development works best with your needs and budget, you can begin to determine your web content. You can start by thinking of your website as a virtual brochure. Your website can contain anything you would include in a handout that you would give to prospective customers.

You need to make sure that hours of operation and contact information for your business are easy to find on your website. You should include details that explain the services or products your business offers and what makes them better than those offered by other businesses. You can include a value statement, something that lets visitors to your website know what you believe in, what you feel is the mission of your company, and what make your business unique when compared to competitors.

Part of this process of informing customers about your business includes reassuring them that you are trustworthy. Testimonials from previous clients can influence prospective clients to give you a try. Similarly, endorsements from partner businesses and links from websites of related businesses will also help promote your business.

You should consider various options for securely handling online payments. You can build a custom interface or use one of the well-accepted options like PayPal or Google Wallet for this purpose.

So far we have talked about what you need to include in the website for your target customers. The website can also be helpful to you in operating your business. For example, you can use it to create a database of client contacts and their information. Along with keeping a record of clients' addresses and buying history, you can start to analyze their buying behavior. Based on your analysis, you could create marketing campaigns targeting specific categories of customers.

Another capability to consider adding is scheduling. Rather than hiring someone dedicated to answering customers' scheduling calls, you can use an automated system where customers can make appointments on their own. This provides customers with more flexibility and it also lowers your costs. But be sure your online scheduling is easy to use for your customers. You want to it to make your business more, not less, accessible.

There are many decisions to make as you plan your company's website. The task can seem daunting. But remember, regardless of which option you select for website development, form should always follow function. The ultimate success of the online storefront lies not in its appearance, but in its functionality. Building an artistic website with a high degree of graphical content may not be sufficient. It is similar to having a lovely book hidden in the library where no one can find it. A successful website should look appealing, but first and foremost it must be well designed for customers to navigate and use easily.

Search Engine Optimization and Search Engine Marketing

As you build the website for your business, you need to keep in mind your primary objective: bringing people to it, so they are aware of what you offer and why they should do business with you.

Earlier we described the fundamentals of Internet search: a user enters keywords, and the search engine finds a list of websites that relate to those keywords. As a business owner, you want your company to appear on the first page of those search results, either through Search Engine Optimization (SEO) or Search Engine Marketing (SEM). We have explained that SEO is the process of increasing the rank of a website or a web page in a search engine's natural, organic search results. SEM (which may use SEO) is a form of Internet marketing that involves promoting websites by increasing their visibility in search engine results through paid search and advertising.

What should you do to optimize your website for search engines? You need to make it easy to access and catalog your website. Your web pages should be suitably titled, so that search engines index them accurately. All the meta-data—or information attached to your web pages but not visible to the customer—should reflect the key aspects of the content of the web pages, making it easy for the search engine to navigate your website.

The key to SEO is not fancy technology, but rather a good understanding of your customer. The critical question you should ask is: "What is my customer going to put into the search prompt when they are looking for a service like mine?" Based on that, you should include appropriate keywords and relevant content in your website as well as in the meta-data associated with it.

As the person most familiar with your business, you are in an excellent position to put together a list of keywords that potential customers might enter into a search. Some search engines also will let you access their databases of past searches to help you predict keywords that may be used. For example, Google has a Keyword Planner tool that will both give you information on the frequency of various searches and also let you know how a keyword may perform in search. You can use this list to generate a set of keywords that you should feature prominently in the content of your website.

With SEO, small modifications to your website can have a noticeable impact on your site's visibility and performance in search results. As we discussed earlier, links back to your website help improve both its popularity and its search engine results rank. So think about ways to increase how many links you have coming into your website. You can use social media platforms like Facebook, Twitter, LinkedIn, and Google+ to encourage people to link to your website. Additionally, you can talk to businesses that offer services or products complementary to yours, and offer to co-market with them. Both businesses will benefit from including links to each others' websites.

Improving your organic search ranking through SEO is only the first step in your Internet marketing strategy. To further improve your visibility in search engine results, you can buy keywords and ad placements in search results. This is called Search Engine Marketing or SEM. In 2012, US companies spent nearly $20 billion on SEM, and the majority of this money was spent on advertising with Google, Yahoo and Bing.

Remember those keywords you included in your web content? For good SEM, you bid on those keywords. The search engines provide you tools to do this, and you can also hire expert consultants to help you. You can think of Search Engine Marketing as a superset of Search Engine Optimization: it improves your ranking in both paid and organic search results.

CHAPTER 6

Attracting and Keeping Customers

In this chapter, we will explain how you can stay on top of your online storefront and make your website a popular and easy-to-find destination for potential customers. This means more than just maintaining your website and keeping it current. You also need to pay attention to how your business is represented in various directories and review sites. You should consider offering promotions and putting in place customer loyalty programs that will help transform clients into long-term satisfied customers willing to give you their repeat business.

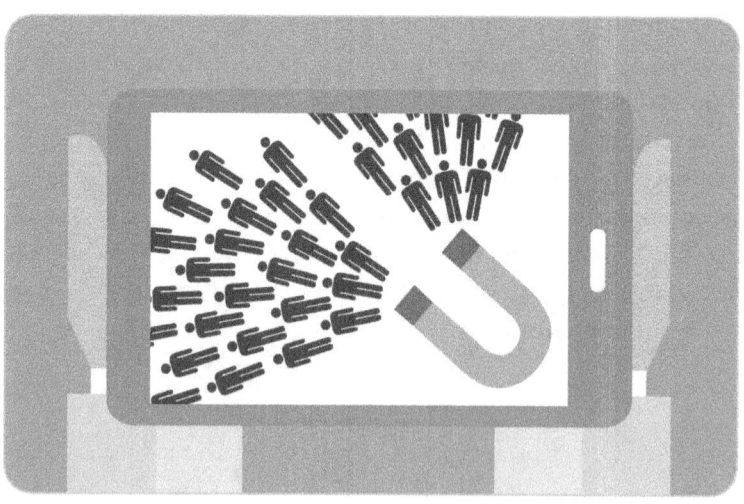

Know Your Business, and Test Your Knowledge

A clear understanding and communication of your business's unique value forms the basis of a comprehensive marketing and sales strategy. This is not a trivial task. The first step is naturally hard, because you need to look at your business objectively and really understand why customers buy from you as opposed to your competition. You have to analyze your competition—both what you can see today and what may be around the corner threatening to change the competitive landscape tomorrow. Many tools exist online that will enhance your ability to understand your company's strengths and target potential customers.

Before you turn to using these tools, outline a clear statement of what you consider to be your company's unique value proposition. Write it down, and then review it with your employees and select customers to get their feedback. Many times the value perceived by the customer is different than you expect—attributes that you value may not be important to the customer, and some elements that you consider trivial could have huge value to the customer. The feedback you receive may make you to shift the focus of your marketing message.

Think about your proof points, or the ways in which you can demonstrate your business's worth. These could be testimonials, customer success stories or industry trends, and you can use them to support your business. If your customers have consistent complaints or concerns, figure out how to handle their objections.

Once you have a good idea about both the unique value your business provides as well as the customer's perspective on it, develop a communication plan outlining how you are going to get this information out to current and future customers. References and testimonials, if seen as fair and balanced, are very powerful. They help potential customers relate to the experiences of other customers similar to them.

Now you are ready to leverage the power of the Internet to your advantage. Maybe your website doesn't place enough emphasis on what your customers value most about your business. If so, be proactive and change it. If you are using a fully featured platform for web development, you should be able to do this yourself. If not, you might need to call your web designer. Regardless of how you do it, you should take the time to have your website reflect what you learn from your customers. A key benefit of an online presence is that you are able to quickly adjust your message to reflect new information. How often have you printed pamphlets promoting your company, only to realize you need to make changes soon after they are printed? An online storefront gives you the flexibility to adjust your message to reflect new data as you receive it.

Customer feedback can be a valuable tool for your business. It keeps your customers engaged and feeling empowered, and it can flag issues to you before they become real problems. On your website, you can set up short surveys to poll your customers and other visitors to your site. People are more likely to respond to something that will take them only a minute or two. The questions you ask could range from the quality of your website, to how your visitors made their decisions to buy or not buy, to open ended questions on what else you could do to improve their experience.

An online storefront creates a more personal and immediate channel for the customer to interact with your business and provide feedback. Your marketing plan should always be adapting to what you learn about your customers and their preferences.

Promotions and Customer Loyalty Programs

Who doesn't love a bargain? Sales, coupons, and discounts have long been used to entice consumers into making a purchase. The Internet has its own versions of buyers' incentives. Companies like Groupon, Living Social, or Amazon Local will let you send promotions to large lists of potential customers. These daily deals are managed through platforms that have their own infrastructure to support direct purchases or coupon redemptions.

You can use these deal-of-the-day platforms to increase your company's exposure to customers, but keep in mind that your online promotion may not result in significant profit. Not only will you be offering a discount to the price of your product or service, but a significant portion of the payment from the customer will be retained by the platform enabling these online promotions.

As a small business owner, you need to consider carefully how these promotions will help you in the long run. If your business thrives on repeat customers—if you own a hair salon or restaurant, for example—a Groupon or Living Social deal can help you attract new customers. When those customers have a good experience with your business, they are likely to come back as full paying clients. If you offer a one-time service with low margins, such as construction or appliance repair, you might choose not to offer a bargain basement price to someone you may not see again for a long period of time.

Bob and Charlotte run a paintball business. "Once we get people to visit us and see how much fun paintball is for everyone, we can get them to come back with their friends. The challenge is to get someone to visit for the first time, and for that we have been using Groupon as a teaser. A family package gets everyone in the facility, and the adventure does the rest."

Managing Your Web Presence

Your website is just the starting point. As a small business owner, you should also be aware of how your business appears on other websites, whether they are online directories, review sites or links from businesses that partner with you. You have to stay current with the reviews on your product or service, and you need to be sure to address negative reviews as quickly as possible.

Make sure you are well represented in directories that your target customers browse. You should do a search of your own company to see where and how you are currently listed. Visit each listing and see if there are any ways you can enhance it. Most Internet directories typically have very basic profiles for the businesses they list. They often allow businesses to "claim" their profiles and add to the information already included there. There may occasionally be a small fee associated with this, but it gives you the opportunity to build a more compelling profile—and one that includes a link to your own website, which in turn improves your website's rank in search results.

Some customers will find you through directories. Others will find you through review sites like Yelp and social media channels such as Facebook and Twitter. Consider giving your customers incentives to review your business in whichever forum they prefer. And be sure to be timely when responding to reviews. Handling negative customer feedback graciously or thanking customers for their positive feedback can significantly improve the perception of your business. You may have observed many hotel managers responding directly to feedback on their properties on Trip Advisor. Many restaurant owners have now started doing the same on Yelp.

Managing Customer Relationships

Customer Relationship Management, or CRM, is focused on managing all interactions with current and prospective customers with the goal of increasing customer satisfaction and revenue. Using a CRM system, you can understand the preferences of your current customers and market new products to them. Selling to an existing customer is easier than trying to sell to a new one.

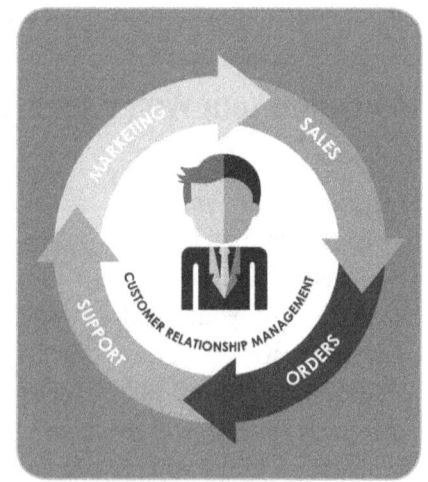

A CRM system provides you with a unified view of all the interactions of your business with your customers. It can organize, automate and synchronize marketing, sales, service and support functions. CRM systems are useful for business of all sizes—the scope and capability will vary based on the requirements of your specific business. For a small business, a CRM system may simply consist of a contact manager that integrates emails, documents, job details, invoices, and scheduling for individual accounts. It tracks customer history and experience, so you can provide your most promising or most loyal customers with the highest level of service.

Most CRM systems are now available on the cloud. Instead of purchasing CRM software, you purchase access to a cloud-based CRM solution such as Salesforce.com. You don't have to worry about owning either the hardware or the software for running a CRM system, and you can access it from your computer or your mobile devices anywhere and anytime. Many CRM systems now integrate social media platforms such as Facebook and Twitter and provide tools to run customer surveys. These additional capabilities will give you better visibility into such things as marketing campaign effectiveness, buying patterns, product preferences, customer satisfaction, and the potential for add-on sales.

At the most basic level, a CRM system helps you understand the buying behavior of your customers, identifying who provides you with the most business, who gives you the highest profitability, and who complains the least or the most. This will lead you to take steps to increase customer satisfaction for your most valuable clients, helping you not only retain their business but also hopefully grow it. You may also decide that business from some high-maintenance clients costs too much time and energy, and you are better served focusing your limited resources on more satisfied and profitable customers.

Data Mining

You can analyze the data collected from a CRM system to improve your understanding of your customers and their preferences. This will increase the loyalty of your customers to your business and reduce the cost of acquiring new customers.

This technique is called Data Mining, and it seeks to analyze customer information with the dual intent of attracting new customers and generating more business from existing ones. Let's say you repair air conditioning systems for homes. A CRM system would help you track the customers you have serviced, how frequently you have done so, what repairs you have made in their homes, and whether they have referred you to other customers. With this information, you could set up your system to prompt you to call existing customers on a regular basis to do an annual inspection or perform a maintenance service.

Bob is a CPA. He has helped customers with their accounting and tax preparation needs for several years. Bob says, "I started using a CRM system a couple years ago. Instead of waiting for customers to call me, I use the CRM database to determine when to set up future appointments. The customers usually thank me for remembering to call them." Now Bob is expanding his business. "I'm starting to offer financial planning services. Using the customer profiles in my CRM system, I have put together a list of customers who may be interested in having me work with them."

Using Social Networks to Your Advantage

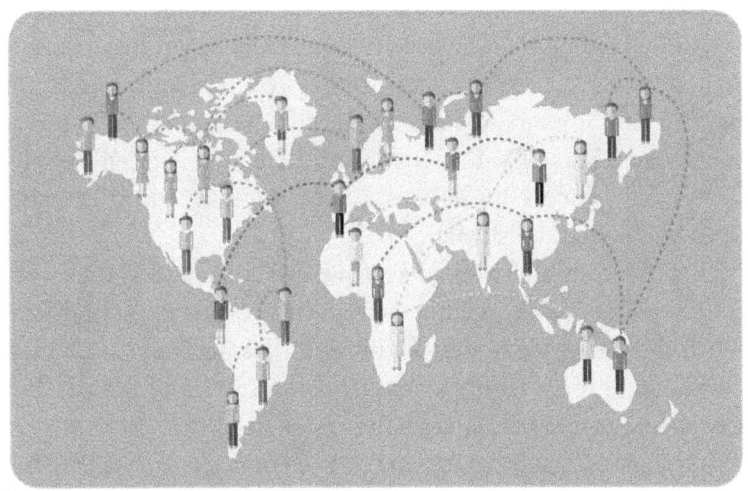

In this chapter, we will talk about how you can use social networks to increase interest in your business. The different networks offer unique advantages, including the potential to advertise on them. You need to evaluate which ones will be most helpful to your business.

Understanding the Different Networks

As a small business owner, you should take advantage of online social networks. To do that, you must first understand some of the specifics of each network you are considering. Who belongs to it? What primary purpose does it serve? How large is it? What information does it ask its members to provide, and how does it store and sort that data? And finally, how can you use the network to your advantage? Let's look at Facebook, LinkedIn and Twitter to illustrate this point.

On Facebook, members create a personal profile. They determine who their friends are, who can see details about them, and who can see the articles they post on their Facebook pages. Your Facebook homepage is set up to resemble a newsfeed, with the news made up of everything your friends have posted to their Facebook pages. Items in a newsfeed can be liked, disliked, and commented on by anyone seeing them, creating ongoing conversations among groups of friends. Facebook tries to predict what members would like to see in their newsfeed, and it filters updates based on these predictions. Interacting with members of your network on Facebook is often described as attending a party—the subject matter is conversational, personal, and full of likes and dislikes.

Facebook also offers an advertising exchange and you can place ads for your business targeting the right type of customer in the right context. For example if a Facebook user has been posting updates about a home remodeling, a general contractor can have ads about his business appear in the target user's newsfeed.

Tom runs a fishing charter service. "People come for the fishing, but it's also about the experience," says Tom. How does he enhance and communicate the value of the experience he offers? "I post a lot of pictures from different trips on my Facebook page, and I tell customers that they should connect with me on Facebook so they can see their pictures. When I tag them in their pictures, the photos pop up on their Facebook pages. They love it, and best of all, all their friends can see the pictures. I get a lot of calls from people who have seen their friends' pictures from my trips and are interested in booking charters of their own."

LinkedIn is organized as a network for professionals. It shares some characteristics with Facebook, such as members having the ability to manage whom they link with and what data is visible to whom. Conversations on LinkedIn tend to focus on professional topics; you will not find funny cat videos on LinkedIn newsfeeds.

On LinkedIn, members identify themselves with their professional interests and expertise. Members can create and join groups, in which people of like interests can share ideas and recommendations with each other. LinkedIn Groups are a good way to gain entry into a community. If your major customers are in the business world, for example if you want to reach lawyers or large company executives, LinkedIn is a good option. If you want to reach yoga instructors, Facebook could be a more effective channel.

Twitter is a network defined by its very short communications. Each post, or "tweet," can have a maximum of 140 characters, making tweets the Internet's version of the one-liner. Unlike with Facebook and LinkedIn, anyone can sign up to follow and receive tweets from another person on Twitter. Businesses often use Twitter to monitor when someone mentions their product or service, gives a compliment, or complains. On Twitter you can also broadcast information about promotions, specials and new products and services to people following your business.

Susan runs a food truck that offers healthy menu items for lunch. She changes the menu every day and goes to different locations at different times of the day. "We use Twitter to let our clients know about the lunch specials and where our truck is going to be. It has been very effective in getting new and repeat customers," says Susan.

Advertising on Social Networks

Before we discuss advertising on social networks, we should also discuss the fact that consumers are now accessing these networks from their mobile devices. As a small business owner, you must be aware of this when building content or creating advertisements. If you build something that is difficult to read or navigate from a smartphone or tablet, you are likely to miss out on many potential customers.

Facebook supports two forms of advertising. Sponsored updates appear in members' newsfeeds and sponsored ads run down the right side of the computer screen. Not all Facebook members are individuals; companies and organizations create "fan pages" to disseminate information and to alert followers about upcoming events and promotions. As a small business owner, you can build a Facebook page, attract fans, and provide them with updates about your company, products or related topics. The tone of these updates should reflect the nature of your company. For example, a CPA will have business-like updates, while a personal trainer may well have more informal ones. Ideally, your fans will like your updates and share them with their friends, thereby exposing your business to thousands of potential customers in the networks of your "fans."

LinkedIn offers similar news-feed capability, though it currently does not support sponsored ads or sponsored updates. Your contacts can "like" and comment on your posts, thus exposing you to people in their networks and providing your business additional visibility.

In a perfect world, whenever you posted updates on your Facebook page or your LinkedIn newsfeed, you could count on your post being seen by all your fans or contacts. It doesn't always work this way. Facebook for example tries to predict what its members want to see, so not every post will make it onto every fan's newsfeed. Also, as newsfeeds are updated chronologically, fans who don't check Facebook regularly might miss your update. In reality, your fans will see less than 20 percent of your updates. So updates are a good means to engage with your existing clients, especially when combined with a newsletter, but they may not help you broaden your customer base.

Advertising on the social networks, on the other hand, is an excellent mechanism to reach new clients. As a small business owner, you can target Facebook members based on location, age, interests, recent posts, and recent comments. You can then pay for sponsored updates to appear in the Facebook newsfeeds of these individuals. These targeted updates let you market to customers who may otherwise be very difficult and expensive to discover. In addition, Facebook provides you with analytical tools that let you understand the effectiveness of your sponsored updates. These can help you improve the effectiveness of advertising on Facebook.

Creating Your Own Business Networks

We are entering the next generation of online communities. State-of-the-art Internet platforms such as Ocoos are building the next generation of virtual communities on the Internet. Small businesses that use the same platform to develop their online storefronts will have an easier mechanism to link to each other. Within a platform-specific virtual community, businesses that provide complementary services can recommend each other and provide space on their website for a partner business. For example a wedding planner can recommend the florist or limousine service she works with regularly. Or the florist can recommend the wedding planner. Each business could also designate a section of their website for promoting their partner business.

The impact of these platform-based virtual communities can be significant. Customers who would have found your business through an Internet search or from review sites like Yelp or Trip Advisor will now be directed to you from other businesses that have already earned their trust. This provides additional value to your customers. Once they have built relationships with one business, they now have "expert" references that they can rely on. These are more valuable than recommendations from unknown consumers on sites like Yelp and Trip Advisor. When they reach your business, they are better-qualified prospects and already inclined to become customers. In this way, all of the networked businesses benefit from each other's marketing efforts.

Overall, these virtual communities create a powerful web of interconnected businesses on the Internet. This helps raise the profile of entire groups of companies in the network and enables these companies to compete effectively against their rivals, both big and small.

Putting it All Together

With many demands on your time, it is easy to put off doing the work needed to market your business online. Hopefully we have shown you that this work is worth doing. And after you have done it, you need to develop habits that will let you enjoy the benefits of creating an online presence for your company. In fact, the one thing worse than having no web presence is having one that is outdated.

Because it is important to manage your web presence on an ongoing basis, we wanted to outline a routine that can work for most small businesses. This will keep your online storefront up-to-date, and it won't require too much time or effort on your part. Think of this as the successful routine of an Internet-savvy business owner.

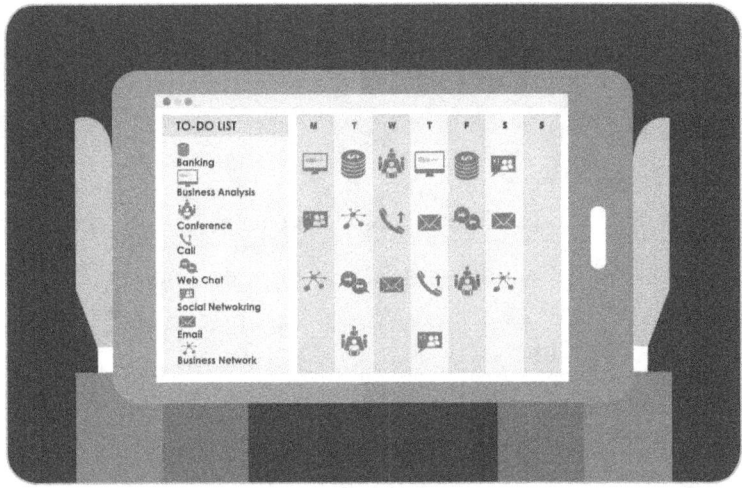

Weekend: (1 Hour)

- Social Media
  - Update social media—Facebook/LinkedIn/Twitter/Business Networks—concurrently.
  - Why? Some of your customers spend a lot of time on social networking sites and this creates new opportunities for your business.

- Web Analytics
  - Review the previous week's visitors to your website and look for trends.
  - Review the effectiveness of any advertising.

- Build Relationships
  - Review previous week's customer list.
  - Write and send thank-you notes to customers and update CRM information.

- Send Reminders
  - Email customers to reconfirm next week's appointments.

- (SEO) Write Blog Post
  - Customer story, industry news.
  - Share blog on social media.

Monday: (15 Min)

- Daily Client Notes
  - Close day and add notes on today's clients.

- Add offline transactions into system for future analysis.

Tuesday: (20 min)

- Social Media
  - Update Facebook/LinkedIn/Twitter/Business Networks.
  - Browse and respond to any posts.

- Daily Client Notes
  - Close day and add notes on today's clients.
- Add offline sales for day.

Wed: (15 Min)

- Daily Client Notes
  - Close day and add notes on today's clients.
- Add offline sales for day.

Thursday: (20 min)

- Social Media
  - Update Facebook/LinkedIn/Twitter/Business Networks.
  - Browse and respond to any posts.
- Daily Client Notes
  - Close day and add notes on today's clients.
- Add offline sales for day.

Friday: (15 min)

- Daily Client Notes
  - Close day and add notes on today's clients.
- Add offline sales for day.

What happens as a result of this routine and these habits?

1. **Better Marketing**: You will enjoy a strong social media presence, effective email marketing, and timely customer follow-ups.
2. **Smarter Business**: You will gain insight into how your marketing is working, knowledge on what is driving online traffic to your

business, and information on sales data including which dates, times and customers are most valuable.

3. **Loyal Customers:** Tracking notes will provide you with better knowledge of your customers. Weekly, monthly or yearly follow-ups and reconnection will boost customer retention and repeat business. Service reminders will reduce missed opportunity. All of these lead to better time management.

4. **Improved Search Engine rankings:** Just one blog post per week will create 52 pages on the web related to your business and help improve search engine rankings.

CONCLUSION

We know that many businesses are still not taking advantage of the opportunities and capabilities that currently exist online. We built the Ocoos platform to provide an easy means for small business owners to get online and capitalize on opportunities created by the Internet. We wrote this book to explain what some of these opportunities and capabilities were and then to detail how you could deploy them in your business.

Being a little apprehensive of a new technology is understandable. But the Internet wasn't designed to be difficult. It is intended to help make our lives easier. At every point along its evolution, it has moved toward simpler, more accessible ways of doing things. There has never been a better time to go online and start exploring what your business can accomplish.

We have given you the starting points. You now understand the basics of how marketing and finance have been impacted by the Internet revolution. You have learned how people find businesses online and share their feedback about those businesses. You know what questions you should ask yourself when deciding what kind of web presence you need for your business, you understand the options available to you when building a website, and you know how to use social networks to promote your business. You now appreciate all these benefits and are keen to take advantage of them.

There is no reason to delay getting started. Learning any new skill requires some effort, but practice will make it easier. The first time you try to post an update on your business's Facebook fan page, you might be a bit unsure. But as you do it repeatedly, it will become second nature to you and you will start to realize the benefits of your efforts.

When you take your business online, you build stronger customer relationships, you improve your company's visibility, you boost your marketing efforts, and you operate a smarter, more efficient and more profitable business. That is what the Internet can make possible for you.

Appendix I:
The Story of Ocoos

In the foreword, we mentioned that the authors came from the Fortune 500 world, where businesses have a great deal of resources to apply toward word-class sales and marketing infrastructures. We noticed that there were some missing pieces among the tools available for managing a business's online presence. Specifically there were three main gaps from the point-of-view of a small business owner:

1. **Management of Tools**: Several capable point solutions existed, but the functionality was not integrated to make them easy to use for a small business owner.
2. **Complexity**: Many of the products were developed for larger enterprises and incorporated capabilities that were not needed for a small business.
3. **Word-of-mouth**: Small businesses live on word-of-mouth and referrals from other small businesses. There was no product that effectively automated the business-to-business referral process.

Being entrepreneurs at heart, we decided to build a product that addresses the above gaps at an affordable price. The key design choices we made for the product were:

1. **Cloud-Based Web-Application**: For all the reasons we have discussed in this book, we wanted an application that a small business owner could easily access from any device without the hassles of dealing with maintenance. This choice paid off when we ported the application to mobile devices and all our customers automatically had mobile optimized websites.

2. **Simple Method to Create a Web Presence with Integrated Analytics**: We wanted business owners to be able to build their websites quickly and get immediate feedback on customer interest. In the process, we wanted to avoid the complexities introduced by popular template-based solutions, which provide lesser value to the business owner.

3. **Integrate Web Presence with Commerce**: An online presence helps get customers into the store, but ultimately the goal is to conduct business. Thus, we integrated functionality for online payments, online scheduling, online surveys, and digital signing and management of legal documents into Ocoos.

4. **Manage Customer Information**: Customer relationship management is key to tracking and keeping in touch with customers. We wanted to enable a platform where business owners could mine this data effectively to offer repeat and new services to customers.

5. **Enable Business-to-Business Referrals**: We built a patented capability where small businesses could recommend other small businesses (B2B) and that referral was automatically integrated into the web presence of both parties.

6. **Easily Connect to Other Applications**: We designed the platform such that data from it could be easily exported to or imported from applications commonly used by small-businesses.

We have integrated the above functionality on a dashboard from where a small business owner could easily manage the business.

We encourage you to give us a try at www.ocoos.com.

Your Business Online, Simply

Appendix II: Directory of Tools for Managing Your Web Presence

In the book, we have described how to develop an online storefront and leverage the Internet to benefit your business. We have used example of several companies to demonstrate these concepts. This appendix provides a list of companies and tools that could be useful to small businesses interested in going online.

Search/Directory Services:

1. www.google.com
2. www.yahoo.com
3. www.bing.com
4. www.yp.com
5. www.manta.com

Google, Yahoo, and Bing are the most commonly used search engines. All of these offer an extensive infrastructure for online advertising. As an example, Google offers Adwords to plan your advertising campaigns on Google and its advertising network. You can use the Google Keyword Planner to access the database of Google searches. This information is useful to determine and bid for the keywords that would be most useful for your business. In addition to search engines, there are several commonly used business directories. Two of the largest are yp.com and manta.com. Yp.com is an online version of the traditional yellow pages. It allows you to list your business and provides a search capability to your customers.

Domain and Web Hosting:

1. www.web.com
2. www.1&1.com
3. www.godaddy.com
4. www.wix.com
5. www.weebly.com
6. www.Bluehost.com
7. www.hostgator.com
8. www.ipage.com

To create a website for your business, you need to get a domain name (or internet address) and a place to host your website. The companies listed above offer domain and hosting services. Generally, they offer similar services and are not all that different from each other. They compete on brand recognition, which is why you may have seen companies such as GoDaddy invest in "creative" commercials during the SuperBowl.

Deal-of-the-day Coupons:

1. www.livingsocial.com
2. www.groupon.com

The two most popular companies in this category are Living Social and Groupon. Both companies have developed a large pool of subscribing customers, who can purchase discounted deals offered in different cities and countries. These companies could be useful for generating initial demand for your business.

Marketing Materials:

1. www.vistaprint.com
2. www.staples.com

3. www.bestbuy.com
4. www.fedex.com
5. www.theupsstore.com

There are many companies that can help a business owner design and produce physical marketing materials such as business cards or brochures. Beyond the national brands, traditionally there have been many smaller local players that also offer printing services.

Review Sites:

1. www.angieslist.com
2. www.yelp.com
3. www.tripadvisor.com

In terms of review sites, Yelp is most known for restaurant reviews but has now expanded into many diverse categories. Trip Advisor started with recommendations for travel and tourism and now has reviews on many topics. Angie's List focuses of reviews of service providers; unlike some of the other review sites, it has a paid membership-based model. We recommend actively managing your presence in the most popular review sites.

Marketing:

Email marketing:

1. www.constantcontact.com
2. www.mailchimp.com

In terms of marketing, Constant Contact and Mail Chimp offer very good email marketing capabilities. Both offer reasonable starter packages for free.

Surveys and Analysis:

1. www.surveymonkey.com
2. www.mouseflow.com
3. www.kissmetrics.com

Survey Monkey offers a widely used service to survey targeted audiences on topics ranging from market research to customer satisfaction. Tools from Mouseflow can help you analyze user behavior on your website by tracking mouse movements, and Kissmetrics tracks and analyzes conversion of web traffic to paying customers.

Finance:

1. www.intuit.com
2. www.freshbooks.com

The de facto standard for accounting software is Intuit's Quickbooks product. This comprehensive product helps you manage your payroll, payments, withholdings, and many other financial actions. For small businesses, Freshbooks is also a good solution for bookkeeping.

Point-of-Sale Tools:

1. www.square.com
2. www.intuit-gopayment.com
3. www.paypal.com

Square, Intuit, and Paypal offer some of the most popular solutions for point-of-sale credit processing. Some provide a device that can be connected to your tablet or smartphone to enable you to swipe credit cards and make the process straightforward and available at a much lower cost.

Marketplaces:

1. www.ebay.com
2. www.amazon.com
3. www.craigslist.com

If you sell products, EBay and Amazon have a world-class infrastructure to showcase your products, enable purchases and payments as well as warehousing and shipping. They are able to offer these capabilities at a fraction of the cost of selling through traditional retailers like Walmart or Best Buy. Craigslist is a very effective alternative to newspaper listings for classifieds – it is local to cities or regions and searchable.

Productivity:

General Applications:

1. Office 365 from Microsoft
2. Google Apps

For basic productivity applications (email, presentation, documents, spreadsheets), Microsoft and Google offer compelling solutions.

Storage/Sharing:

1. www.dropbox.com
2. www.google.com/drive
3. www.box.net

Dropbox offers file storage and sharing services. This is a capability that is very useful for sharing data between several devices and users. Google offers a similar service with Google Drive. Box.com offers capabilities similar to Dropbox.

Communication:

1. www.join.me
2. www.webex.com
3. www.gotomeeting.com
4. www.skype.com

Finally, companies ranging from Join.com to Skype offer excellent teleconferencing and screen sharing services. Most of the services are available for free in a starter package.

Marketplaces for business services:

1. www.elance.com
2. www.odesk.com
3. www.alibaba.com

These are large supplier networks that can help you get stuff done. Elance and Odesk are excellent sources to find various types of services. Alibaba is the powerhouse to access Chinese manufacturing suppliers.

About the Authors

Rahul Razdan has over 25 years executive management experience in a variety of roles in sales, R&D, and marketing. Currently, he is the CEO of Ocoos, after successful exits from PwrLite (Board Member) and WiPower (CEO). Previously, he worked at Cadence Design Systems, where he was the GM of a $400M division. He has  authored numerous technical papers and is named on 24 issued patents. He holds a PhD in Computer Science from Harvard University.

Pankaj Mayor is a Marketing, Strategy and Business Development executive with 22 years of experience. Most recently he was Vice President at Cadence Design Systems responsible for worldwide marketing and a member of the executive management team. Pankaj has expertise and experience in B2B marketing, product man-  agement, partnerships and alliances, strategy and thought leadership, messaging and positioning, branding, change management, demand generation, field enablement, media and investor relations and competitive analysis. He has a Master's in Computer Engineering from Syracuse University.

Erin Cammann is a freelance writer with a Bachelor's in History from Yale University and a Master's in Journalism from Northwestern University.